Dogs

Chihuahuas

by Connie Colwell Miller

Consulting Editor: Gail Saunders-Smith, PhD

Consultant: Jennifer Zablotny, DVM
Member, American Veterinary Medical Association

Capstone
press®
Mankato, Minnesota

Pebble Books are published by Capstone Press,
151 Good Counsel Drive, P.O. Box 669, Mankato, Minnesota 56002.
www.capstonepress.com

1 2 3 4 5 6 11 10 09 08 07 06

Library of Congress Cataloging-in-Publication Data
Miller, Connie Colwell, 1976–
   Chihuahuas / by Connie Colwell Miller.
      p. cm.— (Pebble. Dogs)
   Includes bibliographical references and index.
   ISBN-13: 978-0-7368-6326-1 (hardcover)
   ISBN-10: 0-7368-6326-5 (hardcover)
1. Chihuahua (Dog breed)—Juvenile literature. I. Title. II. Series:
Pebble Books. Dogs.
SF429.C45M55 2007
636.76—dc22   2005037359

Summary: Simple text and photographs introduce the Chihuahua breed, its growth
from puppy to adult, and pet care information.

Note to Parents and Teachers

The Dogs set supports national science standards related to life
science. This book describes and illustrates Chihuahuas. The images
support early readers in understanding the text. The repetition of
words and phrases helps early readers learn new words. This book
also introduces early readers to subject-specific vocabulary words,
which are defined in the Glossary section. Early readers may need
assistance to read some words and to use the Table of Contents,
Glossary, Read More, Internet Sites, and Index sections of the book.

Table of Contents

Chihuahua   (CHE-wah-wah)

4

World's Tiniest Dogs

Chihuahuas are
the smallest dogs
in the world.
They are not much bigger
than a few apples.

Chihuahuas first came
from warm Mexico.
If the weather is cool,
these little dogs need
to wear sweaters.

Chihuahuas come
in many colors.
Some Chihuahuas
have markings.
Their coats can be
short or long.

From Puppy to Adult

Chihuahua puppies have floppy ears. Their ears stand up when they are about 6 months old.

Chihuahua puppies love
to explore.
They climb and play.
Owners must watch
the tiny dogs carefully.

Even fully grown Chihuahuas need special care because of their size. Owners must help them off sofas and beds.

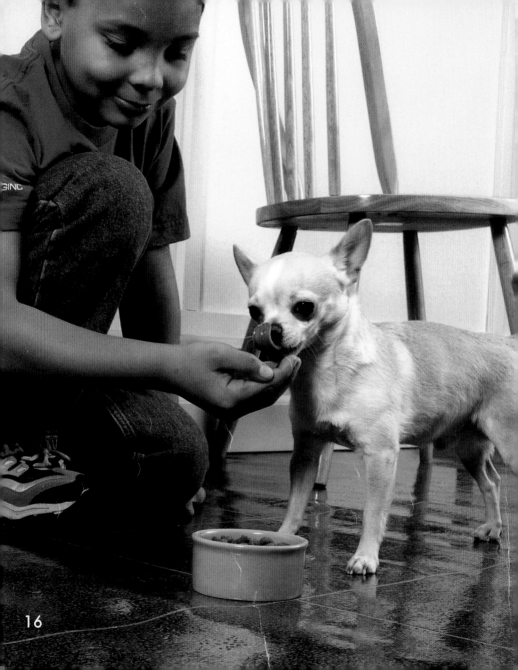

Chihuahua Care

Chihuahuas need only small amounts of dog food and exercise.
But they need lots of attention or they get lonely.

17

Chihuahuas don't need
lots of baths.
Oils in their coats
keep their fur clean.
Owners should brush them
once or twice a week.

Chihuahuas live
about 12 years.
Owners love these little
friends for a long time.

Glossary

attention—playing, talking, and spending time with a dog

coat—a dog's fur

explore—to go searching or looking around

lonely—upset because of being left alone

markings—patches of color on fur

oil—a slippery liquid that does not mix with water

Read More

Temple, Bob. *Chihuahuas.* Checkerboard Animal Library. Edina, Minn.: Abdo, 2000.

Wilcox, Charlotte. *The Chihuahua.* Learning About Dogs. Mankato, Minn.: Capstone Press, 1999.

Internet Sites

FactHound offers a safe, fun way to find Internet sites related to this book. All of the sites on FactHound have been researched by our staff.

Here's how:

1. Visit *www.facthound.com*
2. Choose your grade level.
3. Type in this book ID **0736863265** for age-appropriate sites. You may also browse subjects by clicking on letters, or by clicking on pictures and words.
4. Click on the **Fetch It** button.

FactHound will fetch the best sites for you!   23

Index

Word Count: 158
Grade: 1
Early-Intervention Level:15

Editorial Credits
Heather Adamson, editor; Juliette Peters, set designer; Ted Williams, book designer;
    Kelly Garvin, photo researcher/photo editor

Photo Credits
Capstone Press/Karon Dubke, 14, 16, 18
Cheryl A. Ertelt, cover, 4, 8
Mark Raycroft, 12
Norvia Behling, 6
PhotoEdit Inc./David Young-Wolff, 10
Ron Kimball Stock/ Ron Kimball, 1, 20